I HAVE A
DREAM

DR. MARTIN LUTHER KING JR.

I HAVE A DREAM

60TH ANNIVERSARY EDITION

Forewords and an afterword by Martin Luther King III,
Dr. Bernice A. King, and Dexter Scott King

**MartinLuther
KingJr.** *Library*

Foreword

By Martin Luther King III

On August 28, America will celebrate the sixtieth anniversary of the March on Washington and the "I Have a Dream" speech that my father, Dr. Martin Luther King Jr., delivered on that sweltering afternoon in 1963.

I was just five years old at the time. But I recall that something very profound and powerful had occurred on that day, and the echoes are still reverberating. Indeed, his soul-stirring vision for our country still beckons us to a brighter future for Americans of all races.

I was proud that my dad had given hope and inspiration to so many people. I felt that the work he and my mother, Coretta Scott King, were doing was making America better for everyone.

That day was an uplifting watershed moment for America. Never before had an American leader articulated such an inspiring vision of interracial understanding, goodwill, and even interracial brotherhood and sisterhood.

He said powerful things about the urgency of racial justice for making his dream a reality. He also spoke about the unrivaled power of nonviolence as the only method of social change that could fulfill the dream.

When my dad called for a society in which his four little children would be judged by "the content of their character" rather than "the color of their skin," he was not opposing affirmative action or other compensatory programs, as some have implied to distort his message. Instead, he was saying that we should value integrity, compassion, and kindness and never deny anyone their human rights because of their race.

As we commemorate the sixtieth anniversary of the March on Washington and the inspiring dream my father shared on that day, we are called not only to commemorate his vision but also to correct the festering injustices of poverty, racism, and violence with action.

My father tested his words in the crucible of struggle, and his example inspired thousands of his followers to do the same. That's what gave his words legitimacy. He didn't just talk the talk; he walked the walk.

He understood that leadership is about bringing people together, not tearing them apart. Great leaders build bridges, not walls. They build bridges of hope and opportunity. They build bridges of greater understanding, cooperation, and goodwill. Wall builders marinate in fear and suspicion, but bridge builders have vision. They leverage the good in people that can lead to a better future for everyone.

Despite the significant progress we have made in some areas since the day of the dream, for too many Americans the challenges they face each day— inadequate opportunities to escape conditions of poverty, joblessness, discrimination, social neglect, and violence—have more in common with a nightmare.

Sixty years later, African Americans have even more reasons to fear racially motivated violence, as evidenced by the mass shootings and police violence of recent years. We must restore freedom from fear of violence throughout the nation to help fulfill the dream.

We must ask: What kind of society are we creating when we arm unhinged vigilantes to murder and maim unarmed citizens of all races with weapons of mass murder? The horrific gun violence and mass shootings America has experienced just in this year provide ample testament that there is no way we can fulfill the dream of a peaceful society until we enact gun safety laws. These must include nationwide background checks before the purchase of all guns and a ban on the sale of AR-15-style weapons to the general public. Polls indicate these reforms are highly popular.

And we must address the growing threat to American democracy. The January 6 insurrection and the continuing campaigns to disenfranchise African and

Latino Americans and young people are a direct and immediate threat to free elections. Our challenge now is to mobilize a new coalition of conscience to defend democracy and voting rights in every state.

We are also challenged on this sixtieth anniversary of the "I Have a Dream" speech to support immigrants who come to this country seeking freedom and opportunity. We are called to resist those who vilify or dehumanize anyone because of their race, religion, nationality, sexual orientation, or views on social and political issues. Instead, we must affirm the humanity of *all* people.

As we go forward into the uncertain future, let us remember Martin Luther King Jr.'s challenge to "hew out of the mountain of despair a stone of hope." Let us answer his echoing call to "transform the jangling discords of our nation into a beautiful symphony of brotherhood." Like Martin Luther King Jr., let us be guided by our dreams, not distracted by our fears.

God did not put us all here together in this great nation to shirk our responsibilities to one another or to herd ourselves into racial enclaves or cultural pigeon-holes. We are all children of God, blood of one beautiful family, and it's time for us to honor our identity as brothers and sisters.

As Americans, we will surely continue to disagree about many of the great issues of our times. But instead of allowing ourselves to be dragged down into a polarizing anger and paralyzing hatred for those with whom we disagree, let us instead resolve to disagree as brothers and sisters in a spirit of civility that befits the people of a great democracy.

Let's invigorate our democracy by electing leaders who are willing to reach out across partisan divides to build bridges of trust, cooperation, and mutual respect. Let's elect leaders who understand that real patriotism is not just about revering our heritage, symbols, history, and traditions; real patriotism is about *love* for the people and about serving the people of *all* races, religions, and cultures who make America great. Without that spirit, we will never fulfill the dream. But with that spirit, we will make its realization inevitable.

Foreword

By Dr. Bernice A. King

Did we compromise and diminish the dream to accommodate a more convenient King? If we are to authentically and with integrity remember and contemplate the "I Have a Dream" speech of my father, Dr. Martin Luther King Jr., we must thoughtfully answer this question. On the sixtieth anniversary of the speech, I beckon us to examine how a speech about a revolutionary dream, which was necessitated by the scourges of racism and poverty, is frequently relegated to an emphasis on its triumphant ending without an exploration of its demand for justice. While we have made some progress economically, relationally, and legislatively, we must join together to fully realize the dream that first mesmerized so many six decades ago. We must capture the comprehensive message and, as we do so, commemorate, through compassionate action, the inconvenient dream of an Inconvenient King.

Politicians, preachers, and philosophers often make mention of "I Have a Dream" as though my father were yearning for a type of tragic utopia in which color, ethnicity, and other characteristics that make humanity unique and wonderful have become obsolete. Some will tell you that King wanted us to "not see color." They share on social media that, when he euphorically stated, "I have a dream that my four little children will one day live in a nation where they will not be judged by the color of their skin but by the content of their character," he was telling us to abstain from discussing the devastation and disparities caused by racism.

In doing so, many are invoking my father to justify apathy and indifference. This allows his image and words to be used to denounce and prevent education on racism and its multifaceted historical damage, as well as on its very present danger, both domestically and globally. It is terribly convenient that, as a result of this erroneous messaging about the dream and the dreamer, a leader of love-centered action is misaligned to foster ignorance and to deny efforts to educate children on the persistence of racism. This is especially egregious given that my father, who understood the perilous outcomes of misinformation and social illiteracy, said, "Nothing in all the world is more dangerous than sincere ignorance and conscientious stupidity."

The Inconvenient King did not shun truth in education or promote passivity, and in sharing his inconvenient dream sixty years ago, he was not campaigning for a "color-blind" community. My father was not encouraging mere tolerance or unawareness of one another's ethnicities and heritages but was inviting humankind to move beyond tolerance to love. Love, unlike tolerance, cultivates the best of who we can be and replenishes our wells of compassion and understanding.

The extent to which countless people across the globe have missed this invitation is due, in part, to the often-intentional focus on a more convenient King and on the conclusion of "I Have a Dream." In the thunderous conclusion, we experience the exhortations and expectations for who we can be if we would only do what he methodically conveyed in the previous portions of the speech. Before he told us about the dream, he sought to awaken us to the blights against humanity that warranted his revelation of what a just, humane, equitable, and peaceful nation and world entail.

One of the conditions that necessitated his vision of, and corresponding work for, a "new world" was racial injustice, which, to him, was the "inseparable twin" of economic injustice. As he began "I Have a Dream," Daddy spoke about two documents that are foundational to American ideology and government: the Constitution and the Declaration of Independence. He said that America has defaulted on the "promissory note" within these glorified documents "insofar as her citizens of color are concerned."

In relaying his inconvenient dream, the Inconvenient King goes on to say, "But we refuse to believe that the bank of justice is bankrupt. We refuse to believe that there are insufficient funds in the great vaults of opportunity of this nation. And so we've come to cash this check, a check that will give us upon demand the riches of freedom and the security of justice." Sixty years later, Black people in the United States are still facing the persistent destruction of racial injustice and economic injustice, as evidenced by the racial wealth gap; housing and lending discrimination; health-care disparity; environmental inequity that results in human-made atrocities like "Cancer Alley" in Louisiana and the Flint water crisis; and other manifestations of white supremacist ideology.

My father's statement that "we've come to cash this check" resonates today and is a stark reminder of the indifference in some, and the blatant disallowance in others, for tangibly addressing the dreadful outcomes of racism. In lieu of seeking to repair the economic, psychological, and cultural damage caused by slavery, Jim Crow, and the traumas they birthed, some in our global community find it economically convenient, and conducive for accruing and maintaining power, to compromise the dream.

In addition to being intensified by racial injustice, my father's dream—which seldom meets with the approval of those who desire the convenience of using him to perpetuate their unjust agendas—was also compelled by the urgency of the moment. He said, "We have also come to this hallowed spot to remind America of the fierce urgency of now." The racism and other pervasive evils that haunted our nation then and hound it even now insist that we respond with the understanding that "now is the time to make justice a reality for all of God's children."

Those who ignore the urgency for justice, both in "I Have a Dream" and today, are diminishing the dream and deterring the collective progress that would make justice a reality in the United States and throughout our World House. Similar to wanting to experience the calm that may proceed a storm, the exalters of the prolific ending of the speech, who find it unsavory to co-labor to realize the dream, assert that we have arrived. However, there remains a great work for us to complete together, and we must do so with "the fierce urgency of now" and, as the Inconvenient King said in "I Have a Dream," while conducting ourselves "on the high plane of dignity and discipline."

Further, in expounding on the conditions and the consciousness that necessitated his dream, Daddy spoke about divine dissatisfaction with the perils of injustice and inhumanity. In response to the question "When will you be satisfied?," which he said was being posed to "the devotees of civil rights," he replied, "We can never be satisfied as long as the Negro is the victim of the unspeakable horrors of police brutality." To the dire misfortune of humanity, police brutality is not a relic. In the United States and abroad, the instances of law enforcement perpetuating systemic, psychological, and physical violence, particularly against the Black, brown, and indigenous peoples of the world, are notable and numerous. It has proved to be more convenient to overlook Dr. King's words about police brutality than to highlight his dissatisfaction for the purpose of working on strategic change in public safety policies, culture, and procedures.

The Inconvenient King concluded his statements

of divine dissatisfaction with "No, no, we are not satisfied and we will not be satisfied until justice rolls down like waters and righteousness like a mighty stream." These words, which paraphrase the prophet Amos, are a powerful indication of what my father's comprehensive dream encompassed. His dream was of a nation and world where justice flows legislatively, culturally, and relationally; where leaders are "in love with humanity" and not with money and materialism; where we are not "color-blind" but committed to creating a diverse, inclusive, and equitable Beloved Community; where all children can live without the limitations of discrimination; where freedom (which Cicero defined as "participation in power") and justice (which Daddy defined as "love correcting everything that stands against love") are realities for all.

We can walk and work together to reach this inconvenient dream if we stop diminishing its content and compromising its call to conscience. We can build the will to eradicate the barriers to this vision if we embrace the fierce urgency of now and make our own declarations of divine dissatisfaction with inhumanity and injustice. In his book *Where Do We Go from Here: Chaos or Community?*, Daddy warned us that "the failure to pursue justice is not only a moral default. Without it social tensions will grow and the turbulence in the streets will persist despite disapproval or repressive action."

If we pursue justice, choose nonviolence as the path for our pursuit, and conduct ourselves on the high plane of dignity and discipline, we will avoid what the Inconvenient King called our "violent co-annihilation." And, as he proclaimed in concluding the masterful message about his inconvenient dream, we will be "free at last."

"I HAVE A DREAM"
SPEECH

August 28, 1963
Lincoln Memorial, Washington, DC

I am happy to join
with you today in what will
go down in history as the
greatest demonstration
for freedom in the
history of our nation.

Five score years ago,

a great American,

in whose symbolic shadow

we stand today, signed

the Emancipation

Proclamation.

This momentous decree
came as a great beacon light
of hope to millions of
Negro slaves who had
been seared in the flames
of withering injustice.

It came as a joyous daybreak to end the long night of their captivity.

But one hundred years later,

the Negro still is not free.

One hundred years later,
the life of the Negro is still
sadly crippled by the manacles
of segregation and the
chains of discrimination.

One hundred years later, the Negro lives on a lonely island of poverty in the midst of a vast ocean of material prosperity.

One hundred years later,
the Negro is still languished
in the corners of American
society and finds himself
in exile in his own land.

And so we've come here

today to dramatize a

shameful condition.

In a sense we've come

to our nation's capital

to cash a check.

When the architects of
our republic wrote the
magnificent words
of the Constitution and
the Declaration of
Independence, they were
signing a promissory note
to which every American
was to fall heir.

This note was a promise that
all men, yes, black men as
well as white men, would be
guaranteed the unalienable
rights of life, liberty, and
the pursuit of happiness.

It is obvious today that America has defaulted on this promissory note insofar as her citizens of color are concerned.

Instead of honoring this sacred obligation, America has given the Negro people a bad check, a check which has come back marked insufficient funds.

But we refuse to believe

that the bank of justice

is bankrupt.

We refuse to believe that
there are insufficient
funds in the great vaults of
opportunity of this nation.

And so we've come to

cash this check,

a check that will give us

upon demand the

riches of freedom

and the security

of justice.

We have also come to
this hallowed spot to
remind America of the
fierce urgency of now.

This is no time to engage

in the luxury of cooling off

or to take the tranquilizing

drug of gradualism.

Now is the time to

make real the promises

of democracy.

Now is the time to
rise from the dark and
desolate valley of segregation
to the sunlit path of
racial justice.

Now is the time
to lift our nation from
the quicksands of racial
injustice to the solid
rock of brotherhood.

Now is the time

to make justice a reality

for all of God's children.

It would be fatal for the
nation to overlook the
urgency of the moment.

This sweltering summer of the Negro's legitimate discontent will not pass until there is an invigorating autumn of freedom and equality.

1963 is not an end,

but a beginning.

And those who hope that the Negro needed to blow off steam and will now be content will have a rude awakening if the nation returns to business as usual.

There will be neither rest
nor tranquility in America
until the Negro is granted
his citizenship rights.

The whirlwinds of revolt will continue to shake the foundations of our nation until the bright day of justice emerges.

But there is something that
I must say to my people,
who stand on the warm
threshold which leads into
the palace of justice:

in the process of gaining
our rightful place,
we must not be guilty of
wrongful deeds.

Let us not seek to satisfy
our thirst for freedom by
drinking from the cup of
bitterness and hatred.

We must forever conduct our struggle on the high plane of dignity and discipline. We must not allow our creative protest to degenerate into physical violence.

Again and again,

we must rise to the majestic

heights of meeting physical

force with soul force.

The marvelous new militancy

which has engulfed the

Negro community must

not lead us to a distrust

of all white people,

for many of our white

brothers, as evidenced by

their presence here today,

have come to realize that
their destiny is tied up with
our destiny, and they have
come to realize that their
freedom is inextricably
bound to our freedom.

We cannot walk alone.

And as we walk, we must make the pledge that we shall always march ahead. We cannot turn back.

There are those who are asking

the devotees of civil rights,

"When will you be satisfied?"

We can never be satisfied as long as the Negro is the victim of the unspeakable horrors of police brutality.

We can never be satisfied

as long as our bodies, heavy

with the fatigue of travel,

cannot gain lodging in the

motels of the highways and

the hotels of the cities.

We cannot be satisfied as long as the Negro's basic mobility is from a smaller ghetto to a larger one.

We can never be satisfied
as long as our children are
stripped of their selfhood and
robbed of their dignity by
signs stating for whites only.

We cannot be satisfied as long as a Negro in Mississippi cannot vote and a Negro in New York believes he has nothing for which to vote.

No, no, we are not satisfied
and we will not be satisfied
until justice rolls down like
waters and righteousness
like a mighty stream.

I am not unmindful that some of you have come here out of great trials and tribulations.

Some of you have come fresh

from narrow jail cells.

Some of you have come from areas where your quest for freedom left you battered by the storms of persecution and staggered by the winds of police brutality. You have been the veterans of creative suffering.

Continue to work with
the faith that unearned
suffering is redemptive.

Go back to Mississippi,

go back to Alabama,

go back to South Carolina,

go back to Georgia,

go back to Louisiana,

go back to the slums

and ghettos of our

northern cities,

knowing that somehow

this situation can and

will be changed.

Let us not wallow in

the valley of despair.

I say to you today, my friends,

so even though we face

the difficulties of today

and tomorrow,

I still have a dream.

It is a dream deeply rooted

in the American dream.

I have a dream that one day
this nation will rise up and
live out the true meaning
of its creed: "We hold these
truths to be self-evident, that
all men are created equal."

I have a dream that one day
on the red hills of Georgia, the
sons of former slaves and the
sons of former slave owners will
be able to sit down together
at the table of brotherhood.

I have a dream that one day

even the state of Mississippi,

a state sweltering with

the heat of injustice,

sweltering with the

heat of oppression,

will be transformed into

an oasis of freedom

and justice.

I have a dream that my four little children will one day live in a nation where they will not be judged by the color of their skin but by the content of their character.

I have a dream today.

I have a dream that one day

down in Alabama, with

its vicious racists,

with its governor having

his lips dripping with the

words of "interposition"

and "nullification,"

one day right there in Alabama

little black boys and black girls

will be able to join hands with

little white boys and white

girls as sisters and brothers.

I have a dream today.

I have a dream that one day

every valley shall be exalted,

every hill and mountain

shall be made low,

the rough places will be made

plain, and the crooked places

will be made straight,

and the glory of the Lord

shall be revealed, and all

flesh shall see it together.

This is our hope.

This is the faith that I go

back to the South with.

With this faith we will be able

to hew out of the mountain

of despair a stone of hope.

With this faith we will be able to transform the jangling discords of our nation into a beautiful symphony of brotherhood.

With this faith we will be

able to work together,

to pray together,

to struggle together,

to go to jail together,

to stand up for

freedom together,

knowing that we will

be free one day.

This will be the day,

this will be the day when all

of God's children will be able

to sing with new meaning:

"My country, 'tis of thee,

sweet land of liberty,

of thee I sing.

Land where my fathers died,

land of the pilgrim's pride,

from every mountainside,

let freedom ring!"

And if America is to be a great

nation, this must become true.

So let freedom ring

from the prodigious hilltops

of New Hampshire.

Let freedom ring

from the mighty mountains

of New York.

Let freedom ring

from the heightening

Alleghenies of Pennsylvania.

Let freedom ring

from the snow-capped

Rockies of Colorado.

Let freedom ring

from the curvaceous

slopes of California.

But not only that:

Let freedom ring

from Stone Mountain

of Georgia.

Let freedom ring

from Lookout Mountain

of Tennessee.

Let freedom ring

from every hill and

molehill of Mississippi.

From every mountainside,

let freedom ring.

And when this happens,

and when we allow

freedom to ring,

when we let it ring from

every village and every hamlet,

from every state and every city,

we will be able to speed up

that day when all of

God's children,

black men and white

men, Jews and Gentiles,

Protestants and Catholics,

will be able to join hands

and sing in the words of

the old Negro spiritual:

"Free at last! Free at last!

Thank God Almighty,

we are free at last!"

Afterword

By Dexter Scott King

There are events that occur that are permanently marked in the annals of history and never forgotten. It can almost seem as if time temporarily stood still. On August 28, 1963, seventeen minutes or 1,020 seconds became permanently etched in history. For those seventeen minutes, and the sixty years that have since followed, a speaker captivated the world. He delivered a heartfelt speech that was both a critical retrospective of American history and an optimistic vision of the future. Due to the final five minutes, which are said to have been an off-script ad-lib, it was titled "I Have a Dream." The speaker was Dr. Martin Luther King Jr., who I knew as . . . my father. The speech would become one of the most iconic speeches in world history. It is revered for its ability to inspire, yet also for my father's masterful delivery. It is studied by historians and academics, English teachers and speech professors, and civil rights activists. While the optimistic last five minutes of the speech are the most well-known and often heard, a proper discussion of the speech would be incomplete without reviewing it in its totality. While my father was empowered by the hope and promise of tomorrow, he wasn't so enticed by it that it made him naive to the challenges of the day. Those challenges kept him grounded, while the promise and opportunity for a better future kept him motivated. He was part pragmatist and part aspirational.

I believe the speech is so beloved because of its critical analysis of the conditions of the Negro and race relations in the United States in the 1960s, while also ending on a very optimistic tone that inspired belief in a future full of promise. My father invoked the promises of both the Declaration of Independence, first drafted by Thomas Jefferson, and the Emancipation Proclamation, signed by President Abraham Lincoln. He described the proclamation as both "a great beacon light of hope to millions of Negro slaves" and "a joyous daybreak to end the long night of their captivity." But he noted that some one hundred years after its signing, the Negro was still not free because he was still bound by the chains of discrimination.

He described the Negro finding himself "in exile in his own land." The speech resonates with many and is revered by English and speech experts because of its ability to use words to create metaphors that become as clear as a classic painting. His references to the Declaration of Independence and the Constitution are used to describe America writing the Negro a check, which he has come to cash. He said those documents served as a promissory note, which America has defaulted on. "America has given the Negro people a bad check, a check which has come back marked insufficient funds" was his poignant metaphor. He clung to the promises made in those documents that all men would be guaranteed the inalienable right of life, liberty, and the pursuit of justice. He saw hope and said, "We refuse to believe the bank of justice is bankrupt."

Although my father was a very gifted preacher, he

didn't rely solely on a biblical context for this speech. His intellectual fortitude allowed him to place a mirror in front of America and repeat her words back to her. He was only asking for what was promised to all. This approach was very effective in that it would be impossible for one to say he or she loved America, believed in the founding of this country, and had reverence for our founding fathers, yet did not believe the words they wrote. This speech was not rooted purely in the emotion of the times, but also in the logic of the Negro's argument for equality and justice.

The oft-spoken phrase "History not learned from is bound to repeat itself" has bearing here. To set the stage for his optimism in the hope for a brighter tomorrow, he had to set the foundation of the realities of yesterday and today. We can't advance forward without first acknowledging our present condition. Another reason perhaps the speech has historically resonated so well is because of its prophetic nature. It can be said that the message of the speech not only was timely and addressed the issues confronting our country, but it also was timeless in that it contained universal truths that don't falter with time. The universal truths pertaining to the needs of the human spirit to feel loved, respected, and equal are the same yesterday, today, and forevermore. My father garnered his inspiration from the fact that he truly believed these words: "We hold these truths to be self-evident, that all men are created equal." This gave fuel to his vision that "one day on the red hills of Georgia, the sons of former slaves and the sons of former slave owners will be able to sit down together at the table of brotherhood. . . . I have a dream that my four little children will one day live in a nation where they will not be judged by the color of their skin but by the content of their character. . . . With this faith we will be able to hew out of the mountain of despair a stone of hope."

Mental health professionals have long said that what keeps the human psyche healthy and well is the hope and belief in a brighter tomorrow: having hope in your darkest hour, knowing the sun will yet rise again. Individuals' mental health can be affected when they feel hope is fleeting and all they can see is doom and gloom. The world's recent health crisis, our political climate, and global military conflict being on the rise can give one a pessimistic view of what lies ahead. But like my father, it is imperative that we have a dream of a better day on the horizon. It is the warmth of that promise of a bright tomorrow that propels our spirits forward. Although he thought it very judicious to start with a critical analysis of the history and present status of race relations in our country, he importantly under-stood the need to provide the hope of a more fruitful future, to counterbalance the retrospective tone of the first two-thirds of the speech. As one of the surviv-ing "four little children" my father invoked, it is my sincere prayer that the "I Have a Dream" speech will forever inspire you to keep the faith, keep pressing forward, and understand that the struggle for peace, justice, and equality is one that we can win . . . if we all believe it so.

About Dr. Martin Luther King Jr.

Dr. Martin Luther King Jr. (1929–1968), civil rights leader and recipient of the Nobel Prize for Peace, inspired and sustained the struggle for freedom, nonviolence, interracial brotherhood, and social justice.

About the Contributors

Martin Luther King III is the oldest of Dr. King's two sons.

Dr. Bernice A. King is the youngest of Dr. King's two daughters.

Dexter Scott King is the youngest of Dr. King's two sons.